TINY TERRORS
POISON DART FROGS

JILL KEPPELER

PowerKiDS press

Published in 2024 by The Rosen Publishing Group, Inc.
2544 Clinton Street, Buffalo, NY 14224

Copyright © 2024 by The Rosen Publishing Group, Inc.

All rights reserved. No part of this book may be reproduced in any form without permission in writing from the publisher, except by a reviewer.

Portions of this work were originally authored by Lincoln James and published as *Deadly Poison Dart Frogs*. All new material in this edition was authored by Jill Keppeler.

Editor: Dwayne Hicks
Book Design: Michael Flynn

Photo Credits: Cover Dirk Ercken/Shutterstock.com; (series background) Ruswantodarkness/Shutterstock.com; p. 5 Henk Bogaard/Shutterstock.com; p. 7 Rosa Jay/Shutterstock.com; p. 9 Cuson/Shutterstock.com; p. 10 laksena/Shutterstock.com; p. 11 Paladin12/Shutterstock.com; p. 13 F1online digitale Bildagentur GmbH/Alamy Stock Photo; p. 15 Tanto Yensen/Shutterstock.com; p. 17 alfotokunst/Shutterstock.com; p. 19 Dudarev Mikhail/Shutterstock.com; p. 21 Alberto Zamorano/Shutterstock.com.

Cataloging-in-Publication Data

Names: Keppeler, Jill.
Title: Poison dart frogs / Jill Keppeler
Description: New York : Powerkids Press, 2024. | Series: Tiny terrors | Includes index, glossary, and bibliographic information
Identifiers: ISBN 9781642826302 (pbk) | ISBN 9781642826319 (library bound) | ISBN 9781642826326 (ebook)
Subjects: LCSH: Poison frogs– Juvenile literature
Classification: LCC QL668.E2 K47 2023 | DDC 597.8–dc24

Manufactured in the United States of America

Some of the images in this book illustrate individuals who are models. The depictions do not imply actual situations or events.

CPSIA Compliance Information: Batch #CSPK24. For Further Information contact Rosen Publishing at 1-800-237-9932.

CONTENTS

BRIGHT BUT DEADLY............ 4
WHAT'S IN A NAME?............ 6
ON THE GROUND,
    IN THE TREES................ 8
A FROG'S LIFE................ 10
POISON FOR DINNER?........... 12
TERRIBLE TOXINS.............. 14
THE MOST DEADLY............. 16
FROGGY RELATIVES............ 18
LIVING WITH POISON
    DART FROGS................ 20
GLOSSARY..................... 22
FOR MORE INFORMATION..... 23
INDEX........................ 24

BRIGHT BUT DEADLY

Keep your eyes open if you're ever in the rain forests of South or Central America. What's that flash of color in the middle of all the green? It might be a poison dart frog! These small amphibians come in many colors: bright reds, oranges, yellows, blues, greens, and more. They may have black patterns or spots too.

These bright colors are a warning: don't touch! The skin on some of these tiny frogs gives off a strong poison. They can kill other animals or make them very sick.

DEADLY DETAILS

The poison dart frog's colors are a kind of aposematism. That means animals use their bright colors as a warning to predators that they have poison or don't taste good.

There are many kinds of poison dart frogs. Many are less than an inch (2.5 cm) long.

WHAT'S IN A NAME?

Poison dart frogs have poison on their skin, but they don't bite or sting—or throw darts. They got their name because some native peoples of Colombia, South America, use their poison for hunting. They dip the tips of darts in the frogs' poison. It doesn't take much to take down a much bigger animal.

Although there are more than 100 species, or kinds, of poison dart frogs, only about three kinds are known to be used like this for their poison.

DEADLY DETAILS

All poison frogs are members of the scientific family Dendrobatidae. There are multiple **genera** within this family, including *Phyllobates* and *Dendrobates*.

All the frogs used for poison darts are in the genus *Phyllobates*. This includes the black-legged poison frog.

On the Ground, In the Trees

Most kinds of frogs live mostly in the water. However, poison dart frogs often make their homes among the leaves on the rain forest floor. A few kinds live in trees. Sometimes they climb as far as 32.8 feet (10 m) up! They may spend their entire life in a tree.

Most kinds of frogs have **webbed** feet for swimming. Again, poison dart frogs are different. They have three or four toes on each foot with no webbing. They're not great swimmers.

The dyeing poison dart frog, like some other poison dart frogs, has sticky pads on its toes to help it climb.

A FROG'S LIFE

Poison dart frogs take care of their young. Often, it's the male frogs that stick around and guard the eggs after the females lay them on the forest floor. They'll make sure the eggs don't dry out. There could be one to 40 eggs depending on the kind of frog.

DEADLY DETAILS

Sometimes, the tadpoles will live in water at the center of a plant called a bromeliad. Bromeliads have many leaves growing out of a single base.

Poison dart frog tadpoles will grow into frogs over the next few months.

The eggs will **hatch** in about 10 to 18 days. One of the parents will allow the tadpoles to squirm onto its back. It will carry the babies to a small pool of water.

POISON FOR DINNER?

A poison dart frog eats small bugs, including ants, flies, beetles, and termites. Scientists think that their poison comes from their diet. Some bugs eat poisonous plants, and then the frogs eat the poisonous bugs. This poison doesn't hurt those creatures, but it can hurt many animals that might bother the frog!

Poison dart frogs that live in zoos or other forms of **captivity** don't eat the same bugs they'd eat in their rain forest home. So, these frogs aren't poisonous.

DEADLY DETAILS

Poison dart frogs are diurnal. This means that they're active during the day. Most other frogs are nocturnal, or active during the night.

Poison dart frogs catch their **prey** with their sticky, stretchy tongue.

TERRIBLE TOXINS

Toxins are poisons made by living creatures. Not all poison dart frogs have toxins—but some of those that do are very toxic! If these poisons get into a human's body through a cut or some thin places on the skin, they can make someone very sick—or kill them.

These toxins can hurt or kill predators, so there aren't many animals that will go after a poison dart frog. Their only natural predator is the fire-bellied snake. It has a **resistance** to their poison.

DEADLY DETAILS

All frogs have toxins on their skin. Most, however, aren't strong enough to bother humans.

The green-and-black poison dart frog can be many shades of green. Sometimes it's even more yellow or blue.

THE MOST DEADLY

The most toxic of the poison dart frogs is *Phyllobates terribilis*—the golden poison frog. In fact, it may be one of the most poisonous animals on Earth today. Just one of these little frogs has enough poison to kill 20,000 mice or 10 people.

Golden poison frogs live in western Colombia in South America. They're one of the largest of the poison frogs—sometimes a whopping 2 inches (5.1 cm) long! This may sound silly, but the smallest poison frogs are only about 0.5 inch (1.3 cm) long.

DEADLY DETAILS

The golden poison frog has a tiny range: only about 1,930.5 square miles (5,000 sq km).

Golden poison frogs are often golden or yellow, but they can be orange or green too. They can also have black markings.

FROGGY RELATIVES

The poison dart frogs of South and Central America are often mixed up with frogs in another family—and on an entirely different **continent**! There are many kinds of mantella frogs living in Madagascar, an island off the eastern coast of Africa. They're a lot like poison dart frogs. However, they're not closely related.

Mantella frogs are also brightly colored. They're about the same size as many poison dart frogs. They don't have webbed feet. They're also quite toxic.

DEADLY DETAILS

Mantella frogs and poison dart frogs are examples of convergent evolution. This means that animals that aren't closely related or live in very separate areas **develop** very **similar** features.

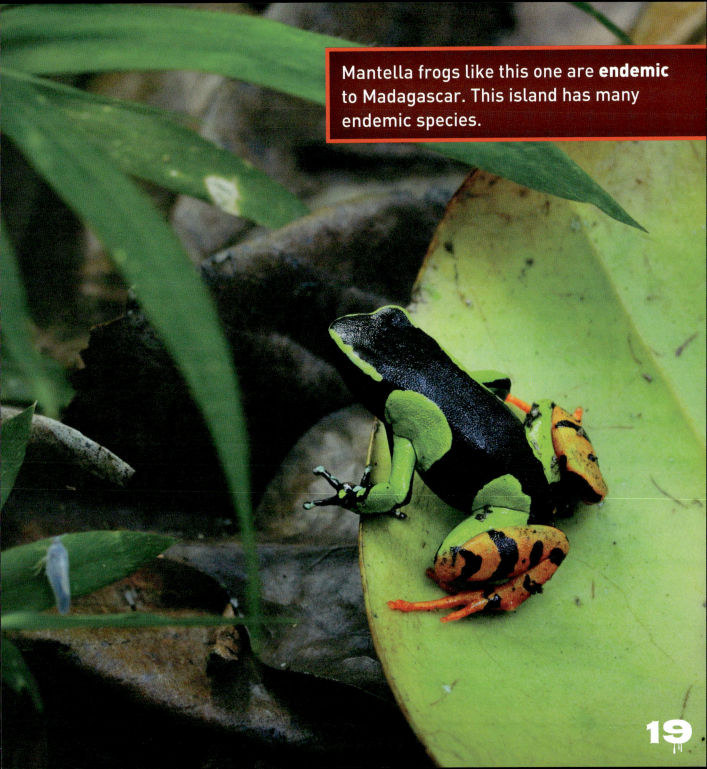
Mantella frogs like this one are **endemic** to Madagascar. This island has many endemic species.

LIVING WITH POISON DART FROGS

As dangerous as poison dart frogs can be, they may also be able to help humans. Scientists have been studying them. Their poisons may be useful as **medicines** for people. They could help with heart problems or pain.

However, some kinds of poison dart frogs are in trouble. People are cutting down the rain forests they live in. Climate change, or change in Earth's weather caused by human activity, is making things warmer. This spreads illnesses that can hurt these tiny terrors.

Some people also take poison dart frogs from their homes to make them into pets.

GLOSSARY

captivity: For an animal, the state of living somewhere controlled by humans—such as in a zoo or an aquarium—instead of in the wild.

continent: One of the seven great masses of land on Earth.

develop: To bring out the possibilities of, to begin to have gradually, or to create over time.

endemic: Growing or living naturally in a particular place.

genus: The scientific name for a group of plants or animals that share most features. (The plural is genera.)

hatch: To break open or come out of.

medicine: A drug that a doctor gives you to help fight illness.

prey: An animal hunted by other animals for food.

resistance: The state of resisting, or fighting against something.

similar: Almost the same or very close to something else.

webbed: Having thin skin between toes or between fingers. Webbed feet help some animals swim.

FOR MORE INFORMATION

BOOKS

Golkar, Golriz. *Poison Dart Frog*. Mendota Heights, MN: Apex, 2023.

Zalewski, Aubrey. *Poison Dart Frogs*. North Mankato, MN: Capstone Press, 2020.

WEBSITES

How Deadly Are Poison Dart Frogs?
wonderopolis.org/wonder/how-deadly-are-poison-dart-frogs
The Wonderopolis web site talks about poison dart frogs.

Poison Dart Frogs
kids.nationalgeographic.com/animals/amphibians/facts/poison-dart-frog
National Geographic Kids provides facts about these colorful frogs.

Poison Frogs
nationalzoo.si.edu/animals/poison-frogs
The Smithsonian National Zoo offers more information about poison frogs.

Publisher's note to educators and parents: Our editors have carefully reviewed these websites to ensure that they are suitable for students. Many websites change frequently, however, and we cannot guarantee that a site's future contents will continue to meet our high standards of quality and educational value. Be advised that students should be closely supervised whenever they access the internet.

INDEX

A
Africa, 18
aposematism, 4

B
black-legged poison frog, 7

C
Central America, 4, 18
climate change, 20
convergent evolution, 18

D
Dendrobates, 6
dyeing poison dart frog, 9

E
eggs, 10, 11

F
fire-bellied snake, 14

G
golden poison frog, 16, 17
green-and-black poison dart frog, 15

M
Madagascar, 18, 19
mantella frogs, 18, 19

P
Phyllobates, 6, 7, 16
predators, 4, 14
prey, 13

R
rain forests, 4, 8, 12, 20

S
skin, 4, 6, 14
South America, 4, 6, 16, 18

T
tadpoles, 10, 11
toes, 8, 9
tongue, 13
trees, 8